Ragi-Ra

Ragi-Ragini

Chronicles from Aji's Kitchen

ANJALI PUROHIT

YODA PRESS

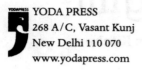 YODA PRESS
268 A/C, Vasant Kunj
New Delhi 110 070
www.yodapress.com

Published in India by YODA PRESS

ISBN 978-93-80403-04-5

Editor-in-charge: Supriya Nayak
Typeset in Dante MT 10.5/15
By Jojy Philip, New Delhi 110 015
Printed at Chaman Offset Printers, Delhi 110002
Published by Arpita Das for YODA PRESS

Contents

Contents

Prologue

Ragi, a much-neglected wonder food has been variously called Nachani, Nagli, Kelvaragu, Mutthari, Coracano and finger millet; an indigenous grain that has been grown and consumed in India's rural areas for centuries. Considering the amount of nutrients it packs in, there is much to warrant making a song and dance about this humble grain. Could it be a mere coincidence then that the two names it is widely known by in India—'ragi' and 'nachani'—carry in them words that denote music (raag) and dance (naach)?

Ragi is a grain that looks like miniature mustard seeds. It is a rich red/orange seed which acquires a fleshy brown colour when ground into flour and yields a pure milky white extract if soaked overnight, ground and squeezed through muslin cloth. This extract is the most nutritious and easily digestible form of

ragi, suitable to be fed even to infants by cooking and mixing in diluted milk. It may, in a manner of speaking, be called the very essence of ragi. The wholesomeness and nutritional value that this form of ragi is capable of imparting not only to the very young, old or infirm but to everyone else in between as well suggests that ragi may well have evolved from the elan vital.

This is a collection of ragi recipes. Some recipes are traditional, some variations of the traditional (in order to make them simpler/faster to cook or to suit the child's palate) and some new discoveries and innovations. Sufficiently influenced by my grandmother's theories, I've never been calorie-conscious: I like to believe that a dollop or two of pure ghee must be used where it must be used. If there is need to cut calories then it is preferable to do that by reducing the size of portions rather than eliminating the fat. That was my grandmother's theory and nobody argued with Aji (or else!).

Before each section in the book there are some 'ovis'. An ovi is a poem in a couplet form—two lines forming a verse—put to an easy tune, which were traditionally sung by women throughout Maharashtra as they went about their chores. This song has helped ease the labour of countless women across the state. In its earlier form the ovi was predominantly about god, mythology, legends and the divine. After the Bhakti movement took root, ovis became more universal and took on broader subjects that included morality, society and day-to-day human experience. Typically, the themes of these songs revolved around the woman's work—her household, the fields, crops, cattle, nature, festivals, her family, children, in-laws and, the topic closest to her heart—her maher (maika or 'mother's home'). The songs speak of her troubles, her joys and sorrows, her wonder at the workings of nature and her rootedness with the earth and the world. Woven throughout these songs of her experience are moral percepts, philosophical musings, a humanistic/heuristic interpretation of the divine, an assertion of the self and a sensibility that reflects the liberalism of the Bhakti movement and the Varkari tradition where devotion to god is incarnate in devotion and respect towards all living beings in the world, nature and life itself. Social bonds are defined in terms of a commitment to the general good and to a very simple morality of shunning greed, avarice, selfishness and pomposity.

The ovis given here are verses by Bahinabai Choudhari (1880–1951), an unlettered woman from the Khandesh area of the state who composed some of the most beautiful poems in Marathi that were at once utterly simple and yet so profound. Bahinabai was born into a comfortable household in the village of Kasoda (Asoda) in the Jalgaon-Dhule area of Maharashtra which for long was known as Khandesh. She was married at the age of 13 into a family that had seen better days and Bahinabai was widowed early in life. Her marital family was one of farmers, so she adopted all aspects of that life as her own. She rose before the sun did, went about her chores and then laboured again in the fields. And while she toiled, she composed couplets in a simple rural dialect about her fields, her land, the soil, every step in the farming process, the implements of work, the well, the grinding wheel, the cow in its shed, the babool tree, rocks, flowers, the human mind, the stove in the kitchen, a match box, god, fate, the blacksmith, the sadhu, the weaver bird and its nest and her own baby, Sopan. Bahinabai never went to school, she couldn't read or write. Yet this unlettered soul composed, in the simplest way, verses that hold truths that are relevant even today.

Bahinabai's ovis were shared by other women like her and

passed down as part of an oral tradition. Eventually Bahinabai's son, Sopandev Choudhari, wrote down as many of her ovis as he could remember. Her poems were first published posthumously in 1952. Today, there will scant be a Maharashtrian household that has not hummed one of her couplets. Her songs have been set to tune in films, they have been recorded and remain hugely popular; her poems are a part of the school and university syllabi and her life and work has been the subject of innumerable PhD theses across universities with a Marathi department.

Interspersing the recipes and Bahinabai's ovis is a rather personal story about Aji, my genius grandmother, myself and the transcendental nachani/ragi grain.

The illustrations in the book are inspired by the traditional implements used in the ancestral Konkani home of Aji and Masi (my mother's sister). Please don't be daunted by these tools and think that ragi can only be cooked with them. The grinding, grating, scraping and pounding that can be achieved by using these grinding stones, scrapers and pounders, can also be achieved, with only a marginal difference in taste, in a modern food processor (Aji surely disagrees!). However, a food processor is not as good-looking so I prefer to sketch the more appealing rustic implements. You are free to take your pick.

– Ragini

Bahinabai's couplets speak of her soil, her work, nature and life. And a large number of them, like the one reproduced on the next page, deal with that which is closest to her heart—her maher (maika or mother's home which is a symbol of unstinting love, eternal welcome, comfort, security and happiness for the woman quietly toiling away in her matrimonial home). Hence the pull of the maher and the joy with which she always looks forward to her visits to the maher, which justifies the eagerness in her step as she hurries to it.

Another verse, 'Majhya Jeeva', is about life, life-force, breath and existence.

Majhya Maherachya Vate

On the way to my Maher

Majhya Maherachya wate
Jari aale payi fode,
Paay chalale, chalele
Ashi Maherachi odhe.

Majhya Mherachya wate,
Jari lagalya re thecha,
Watevarchya dagada,
Tule futali re vacha!

'Neet ja maayabai,
Nake karu dhadpad,
Tujhyach mi maherachya
Vatevarcha dagad!'

Majhya maherachya vate,
Mare salunki bharari,
Majhaya jayachach aadhi,
Saange nirop maheri.

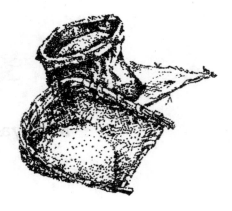

Going to my maher,
Though blistered my soles,
They walk and keep walking,
With that tug at my feet.

Hastening to my maher,
Though I slip and fall,
The stone on which I stumble,
Speaks forth to me and calls!

'Tread carefully, dear child,
Don't hurry and skid so,
After all, I am a rock on the road
That to your maher goes.'

On the way to my maher
Look, that little salunki bird takes wing,
To race me to my mother's doorstep,
And of my arrival sing.

Majhya Jeeva
Life

Aala swaas, gela swaas
Jeeva tujha re tantar
Are jagane marane
Eka Swaasa che antar.

Aike, aike, majhya jeeva
Pidelya che te kanhane?
Dere ganjalyala haath
Teyache aike re mhanane.

Haas, haas majhya Jeeva
Asa sansarat haas
Eeda, peeda sankatacha
Tondavere kale phaas.

Jag, jag majhya Jeeva
Asa jagana tolache
Uccha gagan sarakhe
Dharitri chya re molache.

A breath comes in, a breath goes out
That is the rhythm of life
Between the living and the dead—
The difference is of just one breath.

Heed, listen, oh my soul
To the cry of the distressed
Lend a hand to the weary
Answer his lament.

Laugh, laugh, oh my soul
Laugh so in this world
That you blacken the face
Of affliction and trouble.

Live, live, oh my soul
A life of such worth,
As lofty as the sky
As vital as the earth.

1
Ragini

My name is Ragini. Today I want to make public my romance with Ragi. Though it never really was any great secret, for love has a way of showing itself, in open defiance sometimes, of even the lovers themselves; a sparkle in the eye, a glow in the skin, a spring in the step—it is the humble Ragi that has done this to me. But let me start at the very beginning.

Ma always had a rough time in Dad's house. He, an under-secretary in the civil service, thought he had married beneath his position and treated Ma with the contempt he felt she deserved—an opinion shared by the rest of his family as well. As year after year passed by without any sign of a child being born into the family, Ma began to lose hope of regaining any respect or status within her husband's household. The inevitable followed. She was ordered around, overworked, underfed and often beaten. She would regularly be ill. It seemed they were waiting to see the end of her and, when she hesitantly told Dad she was expecting, no one seemed too enthusiastic or happy.

Late one night, as I sat curled up in her womb, lulled by the song she was softly singing to herself, she suddenly stopped and I felt her muscles contract around me. Dad had come staggering into the room, thoroughly drunk, screaming at her for some reason. Ma just stared at him without answering. It infuriated him further. A short, swift kick to the belly and Ma fell to the floor.

The delivery was difficult. My birth was premature. When they learnt that the child was a girl, they stopped coming to the hospital. Ma died a week later. They wanted nothing to do with me; an ugly runt of a girl with shrivelled-up skin fit only to follow her no-good stubborn mother out of this world. They were only too happy to let Masi take me off their hands and away to her ancestral home in a small coastal Konkan village, Parvi, where she lived with my grandmother, her mother, Aji.

The village doctor shook his head sadly on looking at me but Masi was as adamant as her sister had been. In that house I was reared purely on Masi's grit and Aji's determination and loving care as they nursed me with ragi extract, diluted cow's milk, soft hand-pounded rice and coconut. Day after day they laboured. As a baby they fed me the ragi extract mixed with diluted milk and the starch water from boiled rice. A little older and they made Ragi porridge, then Ragi bhakri (roti), laddoos, seviyan, and a miracle took place. Masi and Aji watched me grow from strength to strength.

Now I am 25, a foot taller than Masi and completing my postgraduate studies in medicine. Colleagues ask me for the secret of my robust health—the shine in my hair, the glow in my cheeks, the nimbleness in my limbs and the stamina that keeps me alert and on my toes almost round the clock—multivitamin supplements? Soya? Uppers? Energy drinks? Eggs and meat? Tonics and herbs? Though all of these may have their benefits, I smile and say it is love. Love for this humble grain that has been cultivated for centuries in my land. Ragi, Nachani, Nagli, Kelvaragu, Mutthari, Coracano, finger millet— all names of the same loved one; rich in calcium, iron, protein and much more. Masi and Aji never knew its exact nutritional value and calorie counts but they knew enough to understand that it would do wonders for that ailing

baby. Here is a way you too can sample the magic. For daily consumption you can mix ragi flour into your regular pancake or roti flour in the proportion 1:3 and proceed as you otherwise would. The ragi will add an unusual heavenly sweetness to the roti. But if you are looking for something a little more exotic then there is nothing to beat the delicacy and simple sophistication of a lesser known sweet from a traditional Konkani household. From the time I was a baby it has been my favourite ragi dish so Masi called it the Ragini Custard. Today I like it still more because even a ham-handed cook like me finds it difficult to go wrong with it. You might find the process a tad laborious but the fruit of your labour is sure to be sweet. If you feel the procedure is intimidating, then you will find an alternative simpler/quicker method at the end of the book called 'Pseudo Ragini Custard'.

THE INCREDIBLE LIGHTNESS OF BEING CUSTARD

Ragini Custard

You need:

Ragi satva (extract) from one cup ragi grain
(Soak the wholegrain overnight, grind well with sufficient water
and squeeze through a fine sieve or preferably through muslin
cloth.) Traditionally, the grinding was done on a grinding stone
but a heavy duty blender can do the job just as well.

Coconut milk, three cups
(One freshly scraped coconut is used. Run it through the blender
till finely ground, add half a glass of water and give it a couple of
more turns. Then squeeze it through muslin cloth or a fine sieve
to get thick coconut milk. Add a glass of water to the residue
and squeeze out thin coconut milk. You may also use packaged
coconut milk if you would prefer that but it will surely suffer a bit
in taste)

Jaggery as per taste (I put ¾ths of a cup)
A generous pinch of powdered cardamom

- Dunk all this in a big pot and cook, stirring constantly till it
  thickens to custard-like consistency. This should take about 10
  minutes unless you have added too much water while making
  the extract. But fret not if you have for then all you have to do
  is a little penance by stirring a while longer.

- Don't think of cheating by putting less water in the first place
  for then the custard will thicken too soon and the ragi will
  remain uncooked. Even if that happens, you must not throw

everything away since ragi is very forgiving and you can stir in
some more water, smoothen out the lumps and continue as if
nothing happened.

- Pour into a lightly greased casserole and allow it to cool.
Refrigerate for 4 to 5 hours, cut into pieces and dig in. The
finished product will have the consistency of firm jelly; the
colour will be a baby pink/light brown depending on the colour
of the jaggery you use.

And the taste? You will surely fall in love as I did. I'm not a chef,
not even a good cook. In fact, I'd best describe myself as a reluctant
cook. But then, love knows no logic, or perhaps it has a logic of
its own and so I am compelled to share this strange fascination
for the grain with you. I believe this grain deserves much more
respect and popularity than it is given. The recipes I share with you
from here on are presented
in an informal way, just as
I remember Aji talking if
I asked her for directions.
She always says, everyone
must work out her/his
own equation with food.
A good dish depends on
so many factors. Practice,
innovation, taste, adjust—
and never forget to add that
intangible pinch of love
and care and serve it with a
generous smile.

There aren't any weights and measures in my recipes. The instructions are more in terms of cups, spoonfuls, pinches and dollops rather than pounds, grams and litres; but they worked for Aji and they work for me, and I hope they work for you too.

2
Breakfast Fare

PANCAKES

In the Konkan they are called 'ghavan'. Popularly, these ragi pancakes can be loosely described as instant dosas.

SWEET PANCAKES

Basic Recipe:

Ragi pancakes are made from ragi flour (who'd ever have thought?). You will need:

Ragi flour, one cup
Sugar, ½ cup
A pinch of salt
Milk

➤ Mix the ragi flour, sugar and salt. Add milk slowly and stir to make a smooth paste (no lumps allowed) of dropping consistency. The pancakes turn out better if this batter is allowed to sit for a while (15 minutes) but can also be made immediately if the kids are getting late for school (or if you're getting late for work) and you want to crack the whip and not let the batter sit around when everyone else is so busy.

- Put a spoonful of ghee/butter/oil on a hot skillet, pour the batter and spread around to form a pancake. If it looks too dry, add some more ghee around it. Cover and cook on low heat for about three to five minutes.

- If the pancake is ready to leave the pan for the dish and is an inviting golden brown, it is done. Fold and serve. If you like them crisp you may turn them over and fry them on the other side though this is, strictly speaking, not necessary.

- You may substitute sugar with jaggery or molasses but then you must use water instead of milk or else the milk in the batter is likely to split. We don't like anyone splitting when we've only just begun!

Variations in Sweet Pancakes

Coconut Pancakes

- Add freshly scraped coconut (one cup) and a generous pinch of cardamom powder to the batter and proceed as above.

Cashewnut/Almond Pancakes

- Add half a cup of roughly (but lovingly) crushed cashewnuts or almonds to the batter. Don't add too much or the pancakes will break.

Honey Cinnamon Pancakes

- Be liberal with the honey and add a dash of cinnamon to the flour. Reduce the milk/water accordingly. Wait and see how the cinnamon spices up your honey.

Chocolate Pancakes

✎ Add either cocoa powder or melted chocolate to the batter. Drop the pancakes as above. Serve with ice cream and strawberries.

These pancakes are heavier than regular ones made with refined flour (maida). If you want them to be lighter, you could substitute part of the ragi with maida. But Aji would consider this sacrilege and so do I. Some people put a pinch of baking powder in the batter. Aji and I don't. Some add Vanilla essence to the batter. We don't. But the ones who do, may.

Fillings

The plain pancakes can also be served with a variety of fillings as might take your fancy. You can make the basic sweet pancake and roll it with these fillings. I am partial towards the coconut filling which is made thus:

Coconut Filling

✎ Roast one cup of freshly scraped coconut for a minute. Add half a cup of jaggery and stir till the jaggery melts. Add raisins, crushed cashewnuts and cardamom powder and stir on low heat till everyone gets intimate (this should take two to three minutes—coconut and jaggery are more sociable than us humans).

(Jaggery can be substituted with sugar, brown sugar or demerara sugar).

Honey-Almond Filling

✎ Peel almonds and grind them into a powder. Mix the almond powder with honey, spread on the pancakes and roll. The pancake rolls are then ready to rock in lunch boxes intended for school or office. Coupled with a wholesome salad it's complete food for the day.

Date-Walnut-Raisin Filling

➤ Chop walnuts and lightly roast. Knead chopped dates and raisins in two tablespoons of castor sugar. Add roasted walnuts and spread on the pancake. Fold or roll over and pack in.

Orange Marmalade or Guava Jelly

➤ If using these oversweet fillings, reduce the amount of sugar in the original batter.

SAVOURY PANCAKES

Since salt is to be added to these pancakes (we can legitimately call them 'dosas' now) it is better to mix the batter with water and not with milk. Some mix it with buttermilk but I prefer to use water. The basic recipe consists of ragi batter made up by

adding finely chopped green chillies and coriander leaves to ragi flour and mixing water slowly into it till it is smooth and without any lumps. Add a pinch each of cumin (jeera), turmeric (haldi), asafoetida (hing) and salt to taste. Rest the batter for half an hour and then pour a ladle full on an oiled skillet. Spread evenly.

Pour some oil all around, if necessary, and cook on medium high heat till the sides begin to come away. Fold and serve with freshly ground chutney.

Variations in Savoury Pancakes

Coconut-Chilli Pancakes

➤ Add half a cup of freshly scraped coconut to the batter along with some more finely chopped green chillies and a pinch of sugar and proceed as above.

Ginger-Garlic Pancakes

➤ Omit the asafoetida in the basic batter and add a liberal dose of grated ginger and garlic to the batter.

Fillings

Make the basic savoury pancake and roll or fold around these fillings:

Coconut-Coriander

➤ Mix together freshly scraped coconut, coriander leaves, chopped green chillies, two teaspoons of roasted sesame seeds, salt, one teaspoon sugar and the juice of half a lemon. Crush and knead the ingredients with your hands so all the ingredients stick together through thick and thin like good friends should. Spread the mix over one half of the pancake just before it is ready to be taken off the heat and fold the other half over it. Or make a thick line of the filling down the middle and roll the pancake.

Onion Filling

- Finely chop two onions (preferably the white ones when they are in season). Add chopped green chillies and grated ginger. You may also sprinkle some red chilli powder or chilli flakes to give it an extra zing.

Sprouts and Paneer

- Mix half a cup of lightly steamed sprouts with two tablespoons crushed paneer. Add chopped green chillies, coriander leaves and the juice of one lemon. You might need to adjust the salt in this recipe to prevent it from becoming too savoury. Add some sugar if desired.

Potato

- Mash two boiled potatoes along with chilli powder, turmeric powder, roasted cumin powder and coriander leaves.

Use your imagination and innovate. The possibilities are endless. Some combinations might go a bit wrong but I guarantee it won't be inedible.

QUICK AND EASY PORRIDGE

This is an ideal breakfast fare guaranteed to keep you on the go till a late lunch without any hunger pangs.

SWEET PORRIDGE

You will need:

> Ragi flour, two tablespoons
> Sugar, two teaspoons
> Milk, ½ cup
> Water, ½ cup
> Cardamom powder, ¼ teaspoon
> Almonds / cashew / pistachio / walnuts, chopped

➤ Add water to the flour gradually stirring so as to avoid lumps. Add milk and sugar. You can add extra sugar if you want it sweeter. Cook for five to seven minutes till the mixture begins to thicken and acquires a glazed look. Add cardamom powder. Pour out into bowls. This can be topped with chopped almonds, cashew, pistachio or walnuts if desired and for added nutrition.

SAVOURY PORRIDGE

You will need

> Ragi flour, two tablespoons
> Buttermilk, two cups
> Salt
> Chilli
> Ginger, grated
> Asafoetida, just a pinch

➤ If you are on a sugarless diet then the above porridge can be made savory by diluting the ragi flour with buttermilk, adding salt, chilli, grated ginger and a pinch of hing (asafoetida) if you like. Then cook as in the recipe above and serve hot.

The gharote, jate or chakki is the grinding wheel traditionally used for turning grain into flour. It consists of two wheels, one placed on top of the other. The lower stone is stationary and the one on top is turned by a wooden handle fixed onto it. A central cavity allows for the feeding of grain into the jate. Sitting at the jate/gharote was a daily activity at dawn when the woman of the house ground the flour needed for the day. While at this job, sometimes in pairs, the women sang these ovis about their lives. This then, is Bahinabai's ovi about the gharote, the grinding wheel—or are they singing about themselves?

The second ovi, Man, is about the intractable human mind/heart, wilful and headstrong like obstinate cattle that will not be herded out of the fields.

The third ovi is about Bahinabai's wonder at the workings of nature as she watches the seeds sprout and grow into standing crop, as though god were a magical snake charmer drawing out the sapling from the seeds buried in the soil.

Gharote
The Stone Grinding Wheel

Kasey gharote, gharote,
Mazhe vaje ghar-ghar,
Ghargharitoon tyachya,
Mala aiku yeto sur.

Tayat ahe ghar ghar,
Yedya, aapalya gharachi,
arey, ahe ghar ghar,
Tayat bharlya abhalachi.

Jashi tujhi re gharote,
Piyu phire gara gar,
Tase doodhavani pith,
Padate re bhuyi var.

Are, gharote, gharote,
Majhe dukhata re haath,
Tase samsara che gane,
Majhe basate mi gat.

See how the grinding stone
Rumbles and whirrs,
And through this whirring,
A tune I do hear!

Fool, can't you hear it?
It's the whirring of our home.
And in it the rumble,
Of the sky heavy with clouds!

As stone spins on stone,
Turning round and round,
So the milky white flour,
Falls gently to the ground.

And at every turning
With growing ache in my arms,
I sit beside you singing,
The song of my samsar.

Are, gharote, gharote,
Tujhyatun pade pith,
Tasa tasa majhe gane,
Potatun yete othi.

Dane dalata, dalata,
Jashi ghamane mi bhijey,
Tujhi gharote, gharote,
Tashi piyu tujhi jhijey.

Jijhisani, jijhisani,
Jhala sangamravari,
Are, tule taklaya,
Takrin aali daari!

Oh, my gharote, gharote,
As the flour from you emerges
So the song in my belly,
From my lips surges.

Milling and grinding
As I am soaked in sweat,
So you too my gharote,
Have worn yourself down.

Grinding, abrading and eroding,
You are now smooth as marble.
So, look now, the takrin's at the door
To chisel and furrow you again!

Man
The Mind

Man vadhaye vadhaye,
Ubhya pikatale dhor,
Kiti Hakala, hakala,
Phiri yete pikavar.

Man mokate, mokate,
Tayale thayi, thayi vaata,
Jashya vaaryane chalelya,
Panyavarlya re laata.

Man lahari, lahari,
Tayale haati dhare kon?
Undarale, Undarale,
Jasey vaara, vahadan.

Man jahari, jahari,
Yache nyare re tantar,
Arey, vinchu, saap bara,
Tayale utare mantar!

The mind, tugs and it pulls,
Like cattle in a standing crop.
Drive it out as you will,
It returns to the field.

The mind, unbridled and free,
Finds escape-ways everywhere,
Like the ripples on water,
Driven onwards by the wind.

The mind, whimsical and frisky,
Who can hold it by the hand?
It frolics and gambols,
Like the wind and the storm.

The mind, lethal and poisonous,
Incorrigible, its machinations.
Better the snake and the scorpion,
A spell reverses their venom!

Man paakharu, paakharu,
Tayachi kaay saangu maat?
Aata hote bhuyi var,
Geley, geley aabhalat.

Man chapal, chapal,
Tayale nahi jara dhir,
Tithey housani veej,
Aale, aale dharti var.

Man yevhade, yevhade,
Jasa khaskhasa cha daana,
Man kevhade, kevhade?
Aabhalat bhi mavena!

The mind, a fledgling, a bird,
Intractable its will.
One moment on the ground
Soaring the sky in the next!

The mind, frisky and spirited,
Not a shred of patience in its hold,
There it turns into a lightning bolt
And falls back to the earth!

How big is the mind?
Small as a single poppy seed.
How large its extent?
Won't fit within the firmament.

Dev Ajab Garodi

God—The Magical Snake Charmer

Dharitri chya kushi madhi,
Bi-biyane nijali.
Var pasarali mati,
Jashi shaal pangharali

Bi tarare bhuyit,
Sarva komb aale var,
Gahivarle shet jasey
Angavarati shaharey.

Oon varyashi khelata,
Ek eka kombatoon,
pragatale don paan,
Jase haath jodisan.

In the womb of the earth,
The seeds are asleep.
As though covered by a shawl of soil
Warm, Comfortable and deep.

The seeds, turgid in the soil,
And the sprouts now push through.
As though, overwhelmed
The earth gets gooseflesh.

Playing with the sun and air,
From each of this sprout,
Emerge two tender leaves
Like hands folded in prayer.

Taalya vajavat paan,
Dang devacha bhajani,
Jase karit karonya,
Howu de re abadani

Kasey varyane dolati
Daney aale gaadi gaadi
Daiva gele re ughadi
Dev ajab garodi.

The leaves clap in rhythm
Rapt in the bhajan
As though beseeching and praying
'Let there be abundance and plenty.'

How it sways in the wind
Grain full by the carts
God has proved to be
A magical snake charmer.

3
Parvi

As far back as I can remember my mornings in Parvi (the village where I grew up) began at dawn to the soft song of the rahaat (the drawing wheel) in the cool dark well in the courtyard. Aji insisted on drawing the water for kitchen use herself. That was my morning alarm. Three buckets, I'd count as the empty brass bucket went rattling down the dark rock-lined walls of the well, a happy splash as it met the water, the rhythmic creak of the rope pulling against the rahaat which accompanied its slow, heavy ascent and then the pouring of the water into copper pots that stood alongside, reflecting the tender morning sunlight, waiting to be filled one by one after which they were dutifully stacked up in one corner of the kitchen. The bath water would already be getting heated over a wooden stove under the neem tree and, after a quick wash, it was time for grinding the grain. Masi and Aji sat on either side of the grinding stone mill, the jate (gharote, chakki). This task always made me feel very important because I had such a crucial role in it. I had to pour fistfuls of grain into the central cavity of the jate as the stone was turned round and round over the grain and the

flour escaped from between the stones in unison with the ovi sung
by the two women at the wheel. Aji was especially fond of the ovis
of Bahinabai.

I was too young to know all the theory and insights contained
in the ovis the women sang, but the easy rhythm of the songs
keeping perfect time with the uniform whirring of stone-turning-
upon-stone coupled with lyrics that were simple, playful and at
times even mischievous streamed so easily into my mind that I
know they will stay with me for a lifetime.

Through the years, as I grew older and faced all the difficulties
and dilemmas that every woman must, one of Aji's ovis would
emerge from an unknown recess of the consciousness and gently
see me through my troubles. It is a debt that I owe to Aji and to
those nameless women of my land who, through the generations,
have preserved and passed down this oral tradition—repeating,
improvising and adding their own experiences to the ovi so that it
was polished into a priceless treasure.

As I poured fistfuls of grain into the central cavity while the
stone was rotated, the rice, wheat, nachni (ragi), jowar or kulith
was pounded into as fine or coarse a flour as was needed on the
occasion. I'd listen attentively as Aji sang one line of the ovi and
Masi completed the next. Sometimes Aji wove my name into a
verse or Masi included some additional lines that spoke of recent
happenings.

My universe, then, for the first 18 years of my life revolved
round a trinity—Aji, Masi and Rege Sir, my teacher in the local
Saraswati Vidya Mandir. Rege 'master', as he was universally
known, was the most respected elder in the whole district. He was
by then very old, even older than Aji. He had taught Ma too. As a
matter of fact, she had been his favourite student. Perhaps that was

why he was partial towards me and overlooked many infractions on my part that he would have sternly dealt with otherwise. My classmates were well aware of this and I was often made a willing scapegoat to shield all of us from the consequences of our juvenile pranks and antics. However, the downside of this benign but sharp gaze was that he also kept a keen eye on my progress and, even if my minor transgressions were overlooked, I knew that there was a strict watch on my academic performance. I wasn't too happy with it then, but I'm constantly reminded of that training at every step in life because this ingrained discipline effortlessly takes me through challenges, academic or otherwise.

Rege Sir taught us Maths and English in the High School and I do believe that I have never met a better teacher. He had studied English at Wilson College in Bombay and was a gold medalist at the University in his postgraduate studies. He was selected for the elite Civil Services during the Raj days but he chose to come back to his Parvi village to teach in the school. He loved children and knew each of his students like the back of his hand. Even if he were to meet them after decades, he not only knew their names and the year they passed out of school but also all their accomplishments, failings, quirks and traits. Rege Sir was known for his insistence on discipline but he was also known for his inexhaustible store of stories; stories from mythology and history, stories of fantasy, magic and of faraway lands and their strange people and customs. When school ended at 3.30 in the afternoon he would sit under the sprawling banyan tree in the corner of the school field and the children would gather there to listen wide-eyed to his tales. Some narrations continued for a week or more and others concluded in an hour. Some were punctuated with poems and songs and others were dramatised by the children who enthusiastically worked with the most rudimentary and imaginative props to enact his wonderful stories. A few of these were then chosen for the annual gathering of the school and it was a matter of great pride for the group whose performance was selected.

School was fun and that 'story hour' the icing on the cake. There wasn't much homework and there were no tuition classes. Evenings passed quickly in improvised games and chatter with friends. Dinner was early, always together and on time. Clearing up didn't take long and after that, for an hour I would listen to Aji's stories before falling asleep on her lap in the warmth of her soft muslin nine yard sari. Aji's stories were not about magic, fantasy, faraway lands or strange people, they were always about just one person—Ma.

When I was a child Aji

told me about incidents from Ma's childhood—what Ma liked to eat, play, read; how she spoke, dressed and wore her hair; the people and places she was fond of and those who took care of her. As a teenager, I still snuggled up before bedtime into Aji's lap and I do so even now to hear of incidents in Ma's life that shaped her character, stories that Ma had come home to relate to Aji about her friends, Ma's plans for her future, the new books she had read, what was being reported in the newspapers, what she'd heard over the radio and what people were talking about. And it was through these nocturnal narrations that I came to meet my mother, Shanta.

4

Mealtime Fare

ROTI

Mix whole wheat flour to ragi in the proportion of three to one. Make phulkas or three fold parathas as you normally make with wheat flour. For the uninitiated, spread the dry flour in a flat-bottomed utensil and pour some water onto the flour. Mix the water and flour with your hands and knead the dough till it becomes a mass but does not stick to your hands. Break bits—about the size of half your fist—off the dough and make into balls. Roll out the rotis on a flat surface with a rolling pin. If the flour is too sticky to roll out, sprinkle some dry flour on top while rolling the rotis. Preheat a tava on the stove, place the roti on it (make sure there are no folds) and

bake on both sides for 5–10 seconds on a low flame. Finally, take the tava off the fire and quickly toss the roti on a high flame. The rotis are slightly brownish but otherwise form a wonderful way to incorporate this grain into your daily staple diet.

Wheat, Ragi and Rajgira Roti

These rotis are made with a combination of different flours which can be mixed together and stored so that you don't have to mix every time rotis are being made.

Rajgira flour, 250 gms
Ragi flour, 500 gms
Whole wheat flour, two kg

(for one-off proportions you mix one spoon rajgira flour with two spoons ragi flour and four spoons wheat flour)

It is said that this combination of rajgira and ragi flour added to wheat offers a complete and well-balanced dish. Adding these grains to the daily roti aata is a good way of incorporating them in the daily diet.

Addictive Additives

It is also helpful to add a tablespoon of jowar or bajri flour to the regular roti atta. Bajri is specially beneficial in winter months. Both add a wonderful crunch to the roti.

Bhakri

Bhakri is a thicker roti made with ragi, jowar, bajri or rice flour. But the method of making these is somewhat different from that of regular roti.

You will need:

Ragi flour, two cups

A cup of hot water

A bowl of regular water (this will help to spread the bhakri on the tava)

A pinch of salt

- Take the ragi flour, add a pinch of salt and make a well in the centre.

- Pour the hot water into the well. Quickly spoon the flour into the water. Mix roughly and cover and keep for five minutes.

- Knead well and divide into portions shaped into balls. (Please note that no oil is added to bhakri dough)

- Back home in the village women make the bhakris by turning this dough into rotis between their palms. It takes a lot of practice to perfect this so I have devised the following method which works fine for me. You can try it too...

- Spread some flour onto the rolling surface and wet the perimeter of the flattened dough with water. Roll out the bhakri with a rolling pin. The trick is that, unlike rotis, bhakris must not be turned over while being rolled. You must roll them only on one side. Also, you will need to roll with a lighter hand than you use for wheat rotis since jowar, ragi and bajri dough is not as elastic as wheat.

Put the bhakri on the skillet and quickly (immediately) take some water in the palm of your hand and spread over the surface of the bhakri. Cook on medium heat for two minutes. Turn over

and cook for a little longer on slightly higher heat. Then turn over again and cook on a very high flame. The bhakri should rise at this stage. Also keep a cloth or flat spoon at hand so that you can seal in the steam if it is trying to escape from anywhere in the bhakri. (Some people carry out this last stage on a direct flame as in phulkas. It's most delicious when carried out on a charcoal chullah if you have one.) Having gotten the bhakri to thus rise to the occasion, remove from heat and serve with garlic chutney/unsalted butter/lemon pickle/onion/mutton or fish curry....or my favourite—freshly churned homemade butter plus lemon pickle/garlic chutney/white onion.

Variations

Fresh Garlic Ragi Bhakri

Remove the threadlike roots and grind the garlic with green chillies, coriander leaves, salt, a teaspoon of ajwain (carom) seeds, cumin seeds and tumeric powder. Mix this chutney into the dough and proceed to make bhakris as above.

If you are unable to make bhakris then this chutney can be similarly mixed in the ragi roti flour and then made into parathas.

Ragi Methi Parathas

Methi (fenugreek) leaves, one bunch, chopped fine

Coriander leaves, ½ cup, chopped fine
Green chillies, three
Jeera (cumin seeds), ¼ teaspoon
Ajwain (carom seeds), ¼ teaspoon
ginger paste or grated ginger, two teaspoons
salt to taste

☛ mix all of the above into roti flour and proceed to make parathas
as usual.

STUFFED RAGI PARATHAS

The stuffing can be made by mixing together

mashed boiled potatoes, cumin, chopped green chilli , coriander
leaves, and salt (to taste)

OR

ground fresh peas
cumin seeds
chopped coriander leaves
salt

OR

paneer
coriander leaves
red chilli powder
salt

Any of the above can be stuffed into the basic roti dough
(wheat+ragi) to make parathas. The easiest way is to roll out two

rotis, spread the stuffing in one, cover with the other and join the ends of the two rotis together by pressing between your fingers. While cooking the paratha, use a few drops of oil on either side to pan fry the parathas. For parathas without stuffing (like the ragi methi paratha on p. 47), roll out one roti and cook on the tava with a few drops of oil. You can either serve the parathas fresh off the stove or roll them up and pack so that they can be carried around and eaten along with mom's mango pickle when hunger strikes.

In the first ovi in this section, Bahinabai speaks of the frugal existence of a house that has fallen on hard times and, as often happens, when there is scarcity it seems to be inevitably compounded by events that make the unfortunate situation worse. The ovi also displays the tongue-in-cheek humour that the poetess often used to highlight the irony of the situation.

The second ovi urges everyone to find God in themselves and their deeds.

Nahi Diya Madhi Tel
There is No Oil in the Lamp

Nahi diya madhi tel
Kashi andharali raat.
Tel miley ekdachey,
Neli undarane vaat.

Vaat keli chindhukichi
Tel diyat padaley
Sapadena aag peti,
Ghode ithe bi aadaley.

Sapadali aag peti,
Aagya vetaala chi lek
Aali, aali haata kaadi,
Laad navasa chi ek.

Shilgavali re kaadi,
Jyot petali, petali.
Andharyala vyabhisani,
Meli eezisani geli!

No oil in the lamp,
Darkness gathers round the night.
At last the oil was found,
The mouse ran away with the wick!

Rolled a shred into a wick
Pour oil in the lamp,
Now where is that matchbox?
The mule—at a standstill again!

Sighted the matchbox,
Darling daughter of the fire jinn,
And in it the single, precious
One and only remaining match stick!

The match it was struck,
The flame burst forth bright,
But, unnerved by the pitch darkness,
She extinguished herself, out of fright!

Dev Disala, Dev Kuthe?

Where Lies God?

Sada jagachya karanu
Chandana pari Ghisala
Arey Swata madhi tayale,
Dev disala disala!

Swata jhala re dagad,
Ghav takicha sosala,
Arey, dagadat tayale
Dev disala disala!

Doley mitaley mitaley,
Swatalebi isarala
Arey, andharyate tayale,
Dev disala, disala!

Male kalaale gupit
Kay tujhi karamat,
Arey, andharane keli
Ujedachya var mat!

Wearing himself out like sandalwood
For the sake of others,
Within himself, then that man
He saw God!

Becoming a stone,
He bore the blows of the chisel,
In that stone, the man
He saw God!

He closed his eyes
Looked beyond himself,
And within that darkness before him
He saw God!

Now I realise the secret
Of your marvel!
How this darkness
Defeated the light!

Dev kuthe? Dev kuthe?
Tujhya bubulya majhar,
Dev kuthe? Dev kuthe?
Aabhalachya aar paar!

Where is God? Where is God?
There, just behind your eyes.
Where is God? Where is God?
He spans right across the skies!

5

Shanta

Shanta, your mother, and Durga, your Masi, were twins, but not identical. In looks, temperament and constitution they were poles apart. Your grandfather named them Shanta and Durga and they grew to be true to their names. Shanta was frail, delicate, shy, studious, serious and quiet. Durga was the tough one—strong, athletic, loquacious and assertive. What bound them together was their love and loyalty to each other. Durga ensured that no one took advantage of Shanta's reticence and Shanta exerted to see that Durga didn't fall back in school. The two of them were joined by Prashant, your Rege Sir's son. The three studied in the same class and were thick friends. Often, if they were not playing outside, then either the girls would be in Rege's house or Prashant would be here, sharing laddoos and pancakes or ragi parathas off the stove with fresh coconut chutney. Yes, the same Dr Prashant Rege who's the head of the Sanjivani Hospital now. They were always together and, together, they were an indomitable team.

Your grandfather was so proud when the girls got a first class in their matriculation exam. He held a feast for the entire village in the temple courtyard. Both the girls were sent to college in Poona where their aunt, my sister-in-law, Shalini Vahini lived. Fergusson College was known not only for its academics but also for the progressive ideas that were taking root among all sections of the people then and Poona, especially the Deccan Gymkhana area, was the vanguard of cultural and political activities. Whenever the sisters came back to Parvi, they'd be full of stories about the meetings, plays, films that they had attended, the powada (street theatre) and revolutionary songs of Shahir Amar Sheikh and Shahir Anna Bhau Sathe, V. Shantaram's early films, the pre-dawn Prabhat pheris (awakening marches) winding their way through the streets of Poona, editorials in newspapers like the *Kesari, Mahratta, Sakal* and the *New Age*, and debates, meetings and discussions among the students about the course the freedom struggle must take. It was a big, new, exciting world that they were witnessing and they were enthusiastically a part of it.

Your grandfather was by now deeply involved in the movement for independence. He had long since resigned his government job at the Taluka Collectorate and become a full-time member of the party. That was when the Swadeshi movement was growing stronger. I remember the time when we lit bonfires in the village ground and he threw his only suit into it. I didn't have any imported saris but I did have a couple of imported lace tablecloths that joined his suit. And the

English tea set that he'd brought for me from Bombay when we were newly married—that went out of our house as well.

He was now required to spend more time in Bombay. The party was organising activities amongst the railway, dock and textile workers there. I think he had taken up a menial job in a textile mill. He had no fixed address and on rare occasions I'd get a postcard saying he was well. From the postmark I gathered that he had also been in Jullunder, a couple of times in Calcutta and once in Meerut. Rege master, who was his friend since their childhood days, was not so actively involved in politics. But he would meet your grandfather whenever he went to Bombay. Rege would always come back with a note from your grandfather and some money. I suspected Rege added from his own pocket to this kitty since he was aware that I was finding it difficult to make ends meet. Rege had even managed to get scholarships for the girls and that eased things to a large extent. I'd have hated to pull them out of college.

Shanta was doing very well in college and was likely to get a scholarship for postgraduate studies at Poona University. She used to write for local magazines. I've kept some of those issues and you can read them sometime. She wrote stories and poems. I think you'll like them.

Durga was the firebrand. She was very active in the Seva Dal at that time. She didn't attend classes but managed to graduate—with more than a little help from Shanta, of course, as usual. Prashant was in Poona too and, after two years at Fergusson, he joined the B. J. Medical College. Durga and Prashant were the ones at the forefront of student activities, organising events, talks, debates, meetings, stage shows, marches and street corner meetings. Through all this, however, Shanta was the reference point for both of them. They knew that if there was a task to be carried out, a leaflet to be quickly drafted, any proofreading or translation to be done, an issue to be deliberated on, a crucial message to be delivered, Shanta could be relied upon.

It was during those days that Durga met Sharad. He was a young recruit in the British army. He was from Yeotmal and came from a family with a strong tradition of serving in the army. I sometimes wonder how they got along. He came from a militaristic, regimented background and Durga had never known what it was to be bound, either in thought or practice. After a short tempestuous courtship Durga came home to announce that this was the man she would marry. I suppose opposites do attract and when I saw them together, their devotion to each other was obvious. Your grandfather was untraceable. I wrote to him at an address at which he'd said I could reach him in case of an emergency. I don't know if the letter ever reached him. Rege too went to Bombay but could not find him. It was a period of mass arrests and summary trials. He had gone underground. Sharad was on a short furlough and his parents had come down from Yeotmal. So, eventually the two were married in a quiet ceremony in the village temple; Rege performed the kanyadaan and Durga went away to Nagpur with Sharad. Over the next three years she shifted four houses as Sharad was posted at various cantonments across the country. She wrote regularly but visited Parvi just once briefly. She seemed happy with her life as a soldier's wife.

Then Sharad was called to serve in France during the final days of the Second World War. Durga came home to Parvi. Your mother was still in Poona completing her studies. She already had an offer of a lecturer's position at the local Wadia College but she was keen on coming back to Parvi to teach in the High School here.

Then suddenly one evening your grandfather was at our doorstep, a bearded, greying man with unkempt hair in a pyjama-kurta. If it weren't for his eyes even I might have failed to recognise him. And when he called out my name, no doubts remained. He was here for three days. Rege had arranged things for him and he had come to finalise the sale of our land outside the village. He hoped to provide for us by doing this. The transaction was swiftly executed and the monies deposited as he desired. There was so much to say and hear in those three days but we barely got any time to talk.

That's how it is my child. So when you have the company of the ones you love, you must seize the moment and hold that precious time close to your heart. Anyway, that's how it was. He said, 'Don't bother asking me what I'm doing or where I am...it changes every two months. Let's talk about you, Sudha, and our two little ones.

Durga seems to be doing well for herself. She's happy and secure. In any case she is the sort who can take care of herself in any situation. But I worry about Shanta. She's growing older and, without a father's presence in the house, I think it would be better if we saw her married into a good household.'

I understood what he was saying. He continued, 'Sudha,

I don't know when I'll see you again. A colleague of mine knows
of a Marathi boy in Delhi. He has just joined the civil service and
they are looking for a match. They will not refuse if my colleague
puts in a word for us. In fact he has already spoken to them and
they seem to be interested. I've given Rege the details and he'll help
with the negotiations.'

'I'll speak to her when she comes home this Diwali', I said.

'The sooner this happens, the better', he said. 'Your finances are
now taken care of. I've given the details to Durga and she'll explain
to you how to withdraw monies from the post office account. If
you need more for some exigency, I've arranged with Rege and you
can take what you need from him. But don't let this opportunity
for Shanta slip out of our hands.'

He left the next day. That was the last time I saw him. Shanta
came home for Diwali full of her usual Poona stories. There were
just a few months left for her to complete her MA in Marathi
Literature. Prashant, now in his final year of MBBS, had come
home too for Diwali and the three friends were together in Parvi
again after so many years. I loved it when the three of them sat
together, all so grown up, and then wolfed down bhakri and bhaji
and steaming hot sewiyan with coconut milk with the same relish
as they had done when they were kids. Prashant and Durga ribbed
your mother about her impending marriage. She only blushed
and looked away. Rege had completed the formalities of matching
horoscopes and the dialogue had been initiated. The family had
liked Shanta's photograph and were impressed by her academic
performance. Things seemed to be going smoothly and I was glad
that your grandfather's responsibilities were being fulfilled. Rege,
Durga and Shanta went to Delhi. No one could have found any
fault with my Shanta. She was the sort who'd fit in, accommodate

and endear herself to anyone. The date was fixed for May and they returned to Parvi.

Shanta grew quieter, if that was at all possible. She stopped going out with her two friends. She helped around the house and did everything expected of her but I could see that there was a sadness in her being. Durga had noticed it too. But we both put it down to the nervousness that every bride feels on the eve of the beginning of a new life with people who are more or less strangers. So we tried to cheer her up in various ways. She'd smile and not say anything.

Oh, Ragini, Ragini, we make such horrible mistakes sometimes. I have never regretted anything in my life as much as not being able to understand my girl then. She had said she wanted to return to Parvi and teach in the school here. I knew Prashant planned to set up practice in Parvi. I knew the two were fond of each other. Then why didn't I put two and two together? Sometimes when the truth is staring you in the face, it is so close to you that you don't see it at all. What I wouldn't give to reverse the course of events! In Shanta's heart was a small dream of a simple life in the village, wedded to her childhood friend, close to her mother, her land and her people, where she could give back to her village what it needed most by working at the school that had made her what she was.

Neither Durga nor I saw it then. Shanta was too shy to speak of her desires, especially if it meant overriding what her father had wished for her. And Prashant! He was too decent to suggest anything different when he saw that Shanta had such an attractive proposal before her. He always wished the best for her and perhaps he thought that he could not give her the comforts that we all believed waited in store for her in Delhi.

Shanta was given away, again by Rege, and she went so very far away from this home.

I waited for those envelopes from Delhi with her small neat handwriting and her letter that always began with, 'Priya aie, saprem namaskar, tujhi nehami athavan yete...' (dear mother, I think of you all the time). She wrote ever so often. The world in Delhi was alien to her. She would write long letters (her language was always so good) about her family there. It seemed to me as though I was meeting them in person every time I read about her husband and her in-laws. She wrote of how sophisticated they were, the very powerful and influential guests they entertained, the amount of food that was cooked every day, her trips to Shimla with Harshavardhan, her husband, his vast circle of friends and the parties she accompanied him to—a lot of what she saw baffled her.

Shanta had been taught to value different things from the ones that were revered in that house. Her sensibilities were different. Her wants were different. She couldn't understand why she must not repeat the same sari at social occasions, why she must not finish all the food that was on her plate, why she must agree with all the statements of certain guests irrespective of her own opinions and laugh with them when they ridiculed beliefs that she held sacred— and so many other such ways of what was called

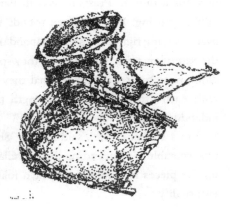

'high' society. She hated wearing make-up and most of all hated going to the club. But then again, Shanta had also been taught to honour her commitments and she would be faithful to the marriage till the end.

She went with Harshavardhan wherever he took her but when it became evident that Shanta was quite unable to adopt all the sophisticated nuances of that 'cultured' crowd, he stopped asking her to accompany him. She would stay back and often, she'd be happiest when there was no one at home. That was the time she could go through those book-lined walls and find solace in some of those volumes, many of which were in mint condition.

It was a year since Shanta had gone to Delhi. Durga was in Parvi since Sharad was still at the front. He was serving in Burma now. A letter from him said that fighting was fierce but he hoped to be relieved for a short while soon and had been given to believe that he would be posted in Deolali for some months. Durga was very happy and I was happy for her.

Then the dreaded telegram came. Sharad was no more. That was the only time Shanta came back home from Delhi. She was here for a month. Prashant was in Parvi too. There wasn't any public grieving. But the three friends went for very long walks every evening right across the ghat and out to the temple on top of the Sateridevi peak. I don't think they spoke much. They probably didn't need to. It was enough that they were together; just being with each other gave them strength to bear the troubles they individually faced.

'I'm a soldier's wife', said Durga. 'Sharad would find grieving unacceptable. I'm proud he died a valiant death. "You must pick up the pieces and soldier on" he'd joke when we spoke of this eventuality.'

And that is what your Durga Masi did. She took up the offer of working in the administrative department in Prashant's small hospital and it has grown to the impressive reputation it has built for itself today because of Durga's untiring efforts and Prashant's single-minded devotion.

Shanta went back to Delhi. Her letters became infrequent. We assumed it was due to her being busier in her domestic engagements. The year was 1947. As the tricolour went up at Red Fort, everyone gathered around the radio at the post office to listen to Nehru's speech. It was as if the entire nation was celebrating a wedding. The air was electrifying, charged with triumph, hope and expectation.

Harshavardhan had been given additional responsibilities at the Secretariat. He had become even more important than before. It had been two years since their marriage and I was looking forward to some happy news from Shanta. But it was only after another four years that she wrote to say very shyly that she was expecting; that I was going to become an Aji.

* * *

Yes, I met my mother in the course of these nocturnal narrations. I came to learn how she thought, what she read, how she spoke, played, sang and wrote. I came to know and love her. But I could never comprehend why she stayed on in that house where she was not wanted, where I was not wanted, where her entire upbringing and value system revolted against their lifestyle. This was a question that would never go from my consciousness. Every time I thought of her, I was tortured by this question.

She came from a family that would have supported her to the hilt; a sister who would stand by her through thick and thin, and a mother who would not, by even a word or thought, question her decision to return. A mother who would have taken her back into the folds of her warmth and supported and helped her stand tall again. She also had a friend who did not commit himself to another woman all his life and who would have been there to help her in any which way. Why didn't Ma tell them what she was going through? Why did she stay on in that intolerable situation?

Yesterday, as I sat by the grinding wheel again listening to the ovi that Aji was singing, I thought I had a glimmer of an answer...

It was an ovi about a woman in her marital home (sasural/saasar) who sings about her mother's home (maher/maika/naihar) while she goes about her work near the fence in the backyard. A sadhu (sage) who is sitting across the fence trying to meditate is disturbed by these constant paeans to her maher and he rebukes her saying:

maze maher, maher, sada gaane tujhya othi
magey maheruni aali, sasaraley kasha saathi?

my maher, my maher, is the constant song on your lips
then why, pray, from your maher did you ever come to your sasural?

To this Bahinabai replies:

> *arey lagale dohale, sange shetateli mati*
> *gatey maherache ganey, lek yeile re poti*
>
> *I feel the dohale (food cravings typical of pregnancy), says the soil from*
> *the fields*
> *I sing of my maher, for my womb will bear a daughter.*

And, Bahinabai continues:

> *dere, dere yogya dhyana, aike kaay mee sangatey*
> *lekichya mahera sathi, maaye sasari nandatey!*
>
> *now listen carefully you yogi, hear what I have to say*
> *So that her daughter may have a maher, does the mother in her sasural stay!*

I think I recognise this ovi. Was this the song that Ma was singing softly to me as I sat curled up in her womb on that fateful night I was born?

6

Tea-time Fare and Desserts

LADDOOS

The Amazing Ontology of the Ragi Laddoo

Thesis: Roasted ragi flour
Antithesis: Coconut,
jaggery / sugar, cashew
Synthesis: Absolutely dialectically delectable laddoo that would
have made Hegel proud.

Ragi laddoos are made with either sugar or jaggery. The ones
presented here contain no water and have a long shelf life. They
don't need to be refrigerated (rather, they must not be refrigerated)
and are easy to carry on long journeys in large steel / brass dabbas
so that you always have filling, wholesome food at hand when
urgent hunger pangs strike and you're on the highway with not a
dhaba in sight.

Nutmeg-Cardamom Ragi Laddoo
(Basic Laddoo Recipe)

You will need:

Ragi flour, three cups
Powdered sugar, 1½ cups
Pure desi ghee, ¾ cup
Nutmeg, finely grated, ½ teaspoon
Cardamom powder, one teaspoon

- Dry roast the ragi flour on low heat till it begins to change colour. This process is best done in a thick-bottomed wok or pan. Keep stirring the flour gently and do not allow it to burn at the base. Add one tablespoon of ghee and continue to turn till the ghee is evenly distributed and the flour becomes a darker brown. Allow it to cool and then mix in the powdered sugar. Make sure that the sugar is not lumpy. (This basic step is common to all laddoo recipes that use powered sugar). Add the nutmeg and cardamom powder.

- Heat the rest of the ghee to just under smoking point. Remove from heat and pour the ragi-sugar mixture into the ghee. (Conversely, you can pour the ghee into the flour—just a matter of relativity as dear Albie would say—same difference). Stir well so as to incorporate the ghee evenly into the mixture which should now be coalescing. Shape tightly into balls (laddoos) using your hands before the mixture cools down. If the mixture is too dry and the laddoos are breaking, grieve not. Just heat and add some more ghee to the mixture. Arrange in a wide plate and show off! Allow the laddoos to cool completely before storing in an airtight jar.

DATE AND ALMOND RAGI LADDOO

You will need

Ragi flour, three cups
Powdered sugar, 1½ cups
Ghee, ¾ cup
Chopped seedless dates, one cup
Almonds (chopped and preferably roasted), one cup
Cardamom powder, a generous pinch

- Add the chopped dates to the chopped almonds and cardamom powder till they are evenly mixed (or oddly mixed but mixed nevertheless).

- Add the date and almond mixture to the laddoo mix (the Basic Laddoo Recipe above).

- Follow the rest of the laddoo-making process described in the Basic Laddoo Recipe.

Fragrant Ragi Singada (Water Chestnut) Laddoos

You will need:

Ragi flour, two cups
Singada flour, one cup
Powdered sugar, one cup
Cardamom powder, ½ teaspoon
Almond powder (lightly roasted), one cup

- Dry roast the ragi flour and set aside.
- Roast the singada flour separately. It roasts much faster so keep a keen eye on it while turning constantly on low heat. Remove from heat as soon as it starts giving out a fragrance so heavenly that you begin to hear violins.
- Mix the singada flour to roasted ragi flour.
- Proceed as described in the Basic Laddoo Recipe.

Jaggery Coconut Laddoos

You will need:

Ragi flour, three cups
Dry or desiccated coconut, grated, one cup
Jaggery, one cup
Ghee, ¾ cup
Cardamom powder, ½ teaspoon
Dried ginger powder, one teaspoon

- Roast the desiccated coconut until it is golden brown and mix cardamom and ginger powder into it.

- Roast the ragi flour and when it starts changing colour, add the desiccated coconut mixture into it. Set aside a tablespoon of ghee and add the rest to the ragi flour and coconut mixture. Mix thoroughly and roast well (for about five minutes). Pour out and put the pan back on the stove.

- Melt the jaggery on low heat stirring constantly. This requires ALL your attention. If the jaggery is overheated then the laddoos will become very hard. When all the jaggery is melted and the spoon turns easily in it, add the saved up spoonful of ghee and remove from heat. You ought to have seen a bubble or two in the jaggery and no more. Do not allow it to caramelise. Quickly add the ragi-coconut mixture to the jaggery and mix thoroughly so that the jaggery is uniformly spread.

- Shape into balls with your hands as described in the Basic Laddoo Recipe and cool.

Bursting with Health, Guaranteed-to-put-the-Pounds-on-Anorexic-Kids Laddoo Mixture

The following ingredients can be added to most homemade laddoos. Individual quantities can be varied according to taste and budget. None of them are compulsory and they have distinct tastes of their own so sugar/jaggery quantities need not be increased only because the quantity of this mix has increased.

For three cups of ragi flour the following quantities are recommended:

a) roasted til (sesame), two tablespoons;
b) poppy seeds, roasted, one tablespoon;
c) methi (fenugreek) seeds, one teaspoon (this adds a mildly bitter taste which gives the laddoo an exotic and interesting flavour);

(All of the above must be lightly dry roasted and ground fine before adding to the flour.)

d) roasted cashewnuts, roughly crushed, ½ cup;
e) roasted almonds, roughly crushed, ½ cup;
(Mamra almonds are considered more medicinal and nutritious than the other variety.)
f) dates, deseeded and chopped, ½ cup;
g) sonth (dried ginger) powder, one teaspoon;
h) nutmeg powder, one teaspoon;
i) dink (edible gum)—two teaspoons—(this is available at your friendly neighbourhood kirana shop. It is in the form of crystals. These must be fried golden in hot ghee and crushed before adding to the mix. It is eaten in winter and is supposed to guard the body against the cold. It is also fed to lactating mothers.);

j) khareek, deseeded, cut into very small pieces, fried and added
    to the 'mix'. Alternatively, it can be finely ground. Some grocers
    offer it in a powdered form;

k) desiccated coconut, one cup. Roast the desiccated coconut till
    the colour becomes golden brown, then lightly crush between
    the fingers. Coconut is a favourite additive, especially in the
    coastal regions, which imparts a divine juicy and delicious
    crunchiness to the laddoo.

Aji, who ought to have taken a patent right on this mix, also adds
a pinch of salt into the flour. She is a covert Hegelian and hence
a firm believer in the unity of opposites. So she says bitter must
always go with sweet and a hint of salt makes the sweet sweeter.
No one can argue with Hegel, or with my gran. So, with a pinch of
salt, bitter sweet it must be (therefore the hint of fenugreek).

COOKIES

The following recipes are rich since they are made without using water, milk, eggs, baking powder or baking soda. These cookies turn out like nankhatai but the method does not involve beating the butter till your arms ache, so they are perfect for the reluctant cook as well as the reluctant-cook-in-a-hurry.

BASIC COOKIE RECIPE

You will need:

Ragi flour, two cups
Powdered sugar (seived to remove lumps), one cup
a pinch of salt
Ghee (this is required to knead the dough)

➤ Mix the flour, sugar and the pinch of salt well. Add ghee, one spoon at a time, while kneading lightly with your hands. Add as much ghee as is needed to form the dough. Do not knead with a heavy hand (Aji used to say, 'A heavy hand always makes tough cookies'). Pat into a greased baking tray (the dough must not be more than half an inch thick) and cut diamonds with a knife, like this:

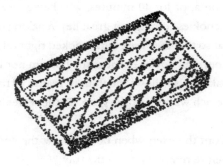

Or squares –

Or, you can cut it into long fingers, like this

Or, you can shape the dough into balls, flatten them and arrange on the baking tray, marking a cross on each one.

Bake in a pre-heated oven at 150°C till the house fills with an irresistable aroma, or for 40 minutes, whichever comes first. The trick to these cookies coming out great lies in baking them on very moderate heat so that they are evenly cooked right till the inside. If made right, they will not be burnt at the bottom nor loose on top. This gentle baking also allows the flour to realise its true potential, basking in the rich warmth of the ghee. So the secret is, 'don't turn up the heat!'

Remove from the oven when done. Allow the cookies to cool completely before removing from the tray.

Variations

Coconut Ragi Cookies

☞ Add half a cup of desiccated coconut and a generous pinch of cardamom powder to the ragi flour and proceed as above.

Cashewnut Ragi Cookies

☞ Add half a cup of crushed cashewnuts to the flour and proceed as above. You can sprinkle some til (sesame seeds) on top of the dough after you have put it in the tray and beat them in lightly with the back of a ladle so that the seeds are embedded into the dough on top. Then cut into diamonds and proceed as above. They turn a golden brown on baking and look good on the deep red/brown of the ragi cookies.

Ragi-Wheat Sesame Cookies

☞ Substitute half the ragi flour with whole-wheat flour. Add cardamom powder and proceed as above. Sprinkle the cookies with a tablespoon each of white and black sesame seeds, beaten in gently with the back of a ladle, and bake as above.

Poppy-Ragi-Jaggery Cookies

☞ Substitute the sugar in the basic recipe with powdered jaggery. If powdered jaggery is not available, then grate rock jaggery and follow the rest of the basic recipe. After you have put the dough in the baking tray, sprinkle the top liberally with poppy seeds. Pat down with a heavy ladle or the back of a bowl so that the seeds stick to the dough. Proceed as in the basic recipe above.

These cookies turn out chewy due to the use of jaggery. You can also add a little desiccated coconut if you like.

Using the basic recipe you can innovate with things like puffed rice, walnuts, cocoa, chocolate chips, rajgira...or anything else that strikes your fancy.

CAKES AND DESSERTS

Ragi flour is much lighter than wheat flour and almost as light as refined flour (maida) and ideal for making cakes. It can be substituted in most cake recipes in place of refined flour. The only difference is that the ragi cake will be more brown and perhaps a tad heavier but that is because it will be stuffed to bursting with vitamins, proteins and iron, among other things.

Here is my basic, no-fuss cake recipe:

Ragi Chocolate Cake

You will need:

Ragi flour, one cup
Castor sugar, one cup
Butter, 100 grams
Cocoa powder, ½ cup
Eggs, three
Baking powder, one teaspoon
Vanilla essence, ½ teaspoon

- Sieve the ragi flour, cocoa powder and baking powder twice and set aside.

- In a separate bowl, beat the butter and sugar till light and fluffy. Add three eggs and incorporate. Fold the ragi mix into the butter mix. Add vanilla essence. If the cake mixture is too thick, add some milk so as to reach a consistency where it will gradually spread if left on its own without support and not sit in a lump.

- Pour into a 9-inch greased baking tray. Even out the top with a spatula but don't thump the tray to get the top even. This is bad for the cake and leads it to sulk and sit down instead of rising to the occasion as it ought to. Bake in a preheated oven at 180°C for 35 to 40 minutes or till a knife inserted in it comes out clean. Turn out. Cool. Decorate if you're feeling creative. Ragi cake has a natural dark brown colour that goes well with chocolate and cocoa.

You can make cakes in different flavours by substituting the cocoa with different ingredients. Add these ingredients once the basic batter is made and mix in gently.

Date And Walnut Ragi Cake

- Add deseeded and chopped dates and walnuts.

Coconut Surprise

- Add desiccated coconut.

Carrot-Ragi Cake

- Add grated carrots.

Banana-Ragi Cake

- Mash two ripe bananas into the batter.

Apple-Cinamon

- Add grated apples and cinnamon powder.

COOL RAGI 'CUSTARD'

This is a variation of the sweet porridge recipe in Chapter 2. Allow the porridge to cool down and add fresh cream. Fold in till smooth and place the bowls in the refrigerator for a couple of hours. The custard will set. It can be eaten as it is or turned out and served with a topping of whipped cream and/or caramel. You can also add cocoa powder to the original mix or pour melted chocolate/chocolate sauce over the set custard before serving.

After pouring into bowls, sprinkle some powdered jaggery, palm sugar or demerara sugar on top. It will melt with the heat and form a faux caramel which tastes delicious in this 'custard'.

PSEUDO RAGINI CUSTARD

This is an easier way to make the Ragini Custard given in Chapter 1. If you find the making of ragi extract time-consuming and laborious, then you can use Ragi flour mixed with water as a substitute and follow the remaining steps to make Ragini Custard. The taste will be compromised a bit but it still remains delicious. Both of these can be stored in the fridge and will stay for up to three to four days.

This custard can also be set in individual cups and turned over in a plate while serving. You can use honey, brown sugar, chocolate shavings and icing as an topping instead of fresh cream. Adding chocolate (blocks, powdered or grated) to the mix while cooking gives the custard a yummy flavour.

Seviyan (Sweet Noodles)

This is a traditional Konkani preparation and is served along with meals.

You will need:

Ragi flour, two cups

Water, two cups

a pinch of salt

Oil, one teaspoon

Milk of one large coconut (don't make this too thin else it will taste insipid. A large freshly scraped coconut should yield about two glasses of milk)

Jaggery, ¾ cup (you can also reduce the quantity of jaggery and add sugar if preferred. The amount can be increased or reduced according to how sweet you like your sweets with no damage to the dish)

Cardamom powder, ½ tsp

- Mix the coconut milk, jaggery and cardamom powder and keep aside.

- Put the water to boil. Add salt and oil. When it is boiling, pour the ragi flour into the water and take it off the heat. Pierce the ragi sitting on top of the boiling water quickly to allow the water to come to the top. Cover and rest for five minutes.

- Pour the ragi mixture out on the kneading surface. Mix thoroughly and knead into a soft dough. Cool.

- Pass this dough through a noodle press and steam the seviyan (noodles) for ten minutes in a steamer.

- Serve steamed seviyan in bowls with the sweet coconut milk poured over it.

When fresh haldi (tumeric) leaves are in season you can use these to impart an unusual, exotic taste to the coconut extract. Just leave a few pieces of fresh haldi leaves to float in the coconut extract.

Alternatively, you can line the surface on which the seviyan is being steamed with these leaves. The slightly earthy, brackish flavour of haldi mixing with the sweet taste of jaggery gives the dish a very uniquely sophisticated flavour (Aji's covert Hegelianism comes to the fore again).

Bahinabai was widowed early in life and was left to bring up her two small children.

The two ovis in this section are composed at the time of her bereavement.

They speak of grief and anguish and then of the determination and resolve that this daughter of the soil rallies in times of such tribulations.

Lapey Karma Chi Rekha
The Line of Fate Lay Hidden

Lapey Karma chi rekha
Majhya kunkavachya khali,
Pusunishi gele kunku,
Rekha ughadi padali.

Deva tujhya gharacha
zara dhanacha aatla,
dhan-rekhe chya charyaney
talhaath re phatala.

The karma line on my forehead
Lay hidden under the sindoor.
When the sindoor was wiped out,
My destiny lay exposed, bare.

God, your fountain of abundance
Has receded and dried up.
The lacerating fate line on my hand
Rips and tears into my palm.

Ata Maza Maley Jeeva
Now My Life is My Own

Arey radata radata,
Dole bharale bharale.
Aasu sarale sarale,
Aata hundake uraley!

Aasu saraley saraley,
Majha malech visawa,
Aas aasava bigar,
Radu nako, majhya jeeva!

Saang saang dharti mata
Ashi kashi jaadu jhali?
Jhad gele nighusani,
Maghe saavali urali!

Dev gele devaghari
Ethey theyisani theva.
Dolya pudhe don laal,
Radu nako majhya jeeva!

I wept and I cried,
The eyes overflowed.
But then the tears receded,
Now only sobs remain!

The tears, they ebbed away,
Now I am my own sanctuary,
Without hope, without tears,
Don't weep, my heart, don't weep!

Tell me, tell me, oh mother earth,
What was this magic trick?
The tree has gone away,
And left its shadow behind?

My god has gone to his home,
And left this legacy here,
Before me two toddlers,
Now don't weep my heart, don't weep!

Radu nako majhya jeeva
Tula radya chi re savay.
Radu hasav re jara,
Tyat sansara chi chav!

Kunku pusale pusale,
Aata urale gondhane,
Tech deyine deyine,
Nashibala aamantrana!

Jari phutalya bangadya
Managati karatut,
Tutey mangalsutra,
Urey galya chi shapath!

Naka naka aaya-baya,
Naka karu majhi keev.
Jhale majhe samadhan,
Aata majha maley jeev.

Now don't weep, my heart,
You have this habit of crying.
Make your tears smile,
That has the flavour of life!

My sindoor is wiped out,
Just the tattoo left on my temple,
That is what will now give,
My fate an invitation!

Though my bangles all be broken,
There is strength in this wrist.
Though the mangalsutra be snapped,
That solemn oath yet survives!

No, no, my good women,
Don't pity me anymore,
Now I am at peace
My life is my own to live!

Epilogue

Both the kids loved train travel, especially the familiar journey from Bombay to the Konkan. It commenced by train from Bombay to Kolhapur with a change of trains at Miraj from broad to metre gauge. After countless glasses of freshly crushed sugarcane juice with ginger and lime, the journey became more fun as it continued for another six hours over a bumpy road through the Sahyadri mountains, with unscheduled stops for gathering wild berries, raw mangoes and fresh cashew fruit off the trees that lined the road. The excitement of the journey was only heightened by the anticipation of reaching their final destination—Parvi village— where they would be pampered by Durga masi and Aji and have a free run of Prashant kaka's huge library of books. I had happily surrendered my 'most favoured' status the day the twins, Venu and Kiran, were born eleven years ago. I have received an abundance of love from Aji and Durga masi and these two kids are so fortunate that they too have this secure shelter in their lives.

Aji brought my dear Ma back into my life by recreating her life and character painstakingly in the bedtime stories that I cherished so much. I met Ma every night and she became part of my existence. Those stories, the articles and poetry Ma had written as a college student and her letters to Aji from Delhi made her an integral part of my being. I came to know my mother and often, as I grew older and faced dilemmas about what I ought to do in difficult situations, it seemed as though she spoke to me. She warned me about decisions, about people and if I nevertheless went ahead and landed in a fix, she gently suggested a way out. When I left Parvi village to study medicine in the big city, it was as if Ma was always with me, telling me to learn from her mistakes, not be dazzled by false pretences, encouraging me to hold my own in a hostile world and to prove my worth through my work.

The hardy Ambassador cab wound its way through the forested mountains interspersed by stretches of rocky plateau—'kaatal'— where, occasionally, just a solitary banyan tree stood guarding the horizon. The rains had been early this year and it was nearing sundown. The air was fresh and cool against our faces. We crossed the plateau and began the descent; the valley below was beautiful, with flights of swallows circling the depths to find a cozy haven to disappear into for the night. And on across the valley was the glimmer of a thin strip of the ocean, lacy and white as it met Parvi village. One by one familiar landmarks made their appearance as though they were waiting at the outpost to greet and welcome. The small stone Sateridevi temple that the three friends would trek to together, the dense foliage aglow with fireflies, night sounds of the mountains, whistling thrushes, terns, egrets, hornbills and barbets, a family of monkeys waiting on a culvert looking to be fed, enormous anthills with burrows, the flash of a green vine viper as it disappears from sight, and all of a sudden on the next turn, before the paddy fields of Parvi could commence, stood the Sanjeevani

Hospital. It stood on a hill, overlooking Parvi, almost like a beacon reassuring the village of its health and well-being. Modest yet spacious, meticulously and proudly tended to by Durga masi and Prashant kaka to a position where it now was a point of reference for all the medical needs of the district. I'd made it a rule to return to Parvi every year and serve at this hospital for two months each time. It kept me rooted to my land and also gave Venu and Kiran the foundation that would keep them grounded and strong. In fact, once we touched the Parvi soil, the children would just disappear—meeting their friends here, being pampered by Aji and Masi—returning only for food and sleep. I believe it to be the sort of holiday they would remember all their lives and which, possibly, just could not be replicated anywhere else.

Dr Prashant Rege had worked tirelessly to build this. His sincerity and dedication to this mission saw the small nursing home grow into a hospital with the best facilities in the whole of the Konkan. Durga masi had proved to be a big source of strength. It was as though they had once again taken up a campaign to bring this dream to fruition just as they had once worked together in Poona to realise their political aspirations (this time though Shanta was not there to complete the triumvirate). Masi oversaw the administration of the hospital with an iron hand. Rege worked to see that the junior doctors were inspired by his vision. Slowly they opened rudimentary medical units in the surrounding villages and within a decade there was a primary health centre in every village of the district and seven ambulances that served to transfer patients to the Parvi hospital when necessary. When the organisation stabilised and its functioning became streamlined and smooth Durga masi shifted focus and took up the work of setting up small home industry units in the area. As of now she has six womens' collective units working in the hamlets surrounding Parvi. The emphasis is, perhaps obviously, on food products made from ragi—papad, seviyan, flour, and dehydrated ragi extract.

It's amazing how quickly two months can fly when you're back home for a rest. But it had been a satisfying 'internship' again at Sanjeevani this year. The kids were upset at the end of their vacation but Aji bribed them with boxes of goodies that she'd made for them to take away.

The rains were early this year. The car sped away leaving tracks in the muddy road leading out of Parvi village. The showers came down, obliterating the tracks the car had tried to leave behind. As the children on either side of me quietly relished the Ragi sweets Aji had made for them, I thought of the decision I had made on this holiday—when Prashant Kaka was ready to relinquish his post at the hospital, I Ragini, would return for good to Parvi.

Glossary

Aata	flour
Aji	grandmother
Ajwain	carom seed (bishop's weed)
Bajri	pearl millet
Bhakri	a thicker flatbread
Bhakti	devotion
Dink	edible gum (gum arabic)
Dosa	pancake
Gharote	stone grinding wheel
Ghavan	pancake
Ghee	clarified butter
Haldi	turmeric
Hing	asafoetida
Jate	stone grinding wheel
Jeera	cumin
Jowar	sorghum

Khareek	dried dates
Kulith	horsegram
Laddoos	ball-shaped Indian sweet
Maher	natal home
Mamra almonds	a variety of almonds distinct from the usual 'American almond', differentiated by its appearance (flattened on one side) and taste (sweeter) that are believed to be more nutritious
Maasi	aunt (mother's sister)
Methi	fenugreek
Nachni	finger millet
Nankhatai	eggless, light biscuit or cookie.
Ovi	verse in couplet form (Marathi)
Paratha	stuffed flatbread
Ragi	finger millet
Rajgira	amaranth grain
Roti	flatbread
Saasar	matrimonial home
Sasural	matrimonial home
Seva Dal	a grassroots organisation of the Indian National Congress with socialist leanings
Seviyan	sweet vermicelli dish
Sonth	dried ginger powder
Tava	flat or convex disc-shaped griddle
Til	sesame
Varkari	a pilgrim. In Maharashtra the Varkari tradition (or movement) originated in the thirteenth century. The movement was influenced by the philosophy of Bhakti and advocated a liberal, inclusive and egalitarian form of worship.

Author's Note

I dedicate this book to the three women in my life—Aji and Tai (my two grandmothers) and Aie (my mother).

Aji, who hid nerves of steel beneath a countenance of serene equanimity. Whose composure and resolve saw her through the harshest of circumstances and whose intense loyalty towards the ones she loved never wavered nor weakened even until her final breath. Aji, whose views on and understanding of life, people, society, even politics held a native wit and sharp insight that went far beyond her time.

Tai, whose mercurial temper and intractable obstinacy were rivalled only by her free-handed, impulsive and uncalculating generosity. This prodigal daughter of Khandesh would give till it hurt and never feel it. Tai, for whom prosperity only meant that she had that much more to give away.

Aie, a bundle of contradictions. So fragile and yet so strong, vulnerable and stoic, outspoken and reticent, irrational, unreasonable, demanding and then so giving, tender and loving. Each little quarrel we might have had over the years has brought us even closer together, so close now that it feels as thought we are to each other the sister neither of us had.

And all these three women, in their own very different ways, have shared one trait in common. All their life they have nurtured and kept alive the child in them. The child who will never give up on illusions and dreams, who trusts, loves and hopes—that child who is the best insulation against all the bitterness, betrayal and perfidy that life might attempt to cast our way.

Anjali Purohit
December 2011